PRAYER. AFFIRMATION. GRATITUDE.
EXHALING. SILENCE

RESILIENCE

MAKING LIFE WORTH LIVING

DR. MICHAEL A. CHAMBERS

DEDICATION

To God Be the Glory For the great things He has done for my family and me. A life filled with extraordinary blessings and seasons of impediments. To that end, I give all praises to Jesus Christ. Additionally, I dedicate this book to my loving wife of 23 years, Lizzie and my children: Nicholas and Nykia for their endless love, indisputable resilience and unfathomable support through many years of pastoral assignments, ministry commitments and business ventures. Furthermore, I am eternally indebted to my wife, Lizzie for being such a lady of grace and teaching me the significance of quite strength. I praise God for my two oldest Aja, Sean and grandson Sean Tavarious. I pray this work will serve as a testament of my walk with God to them and my entire family.

I offer my profound gratitude to my mother Virginia McGee and the late David McGee, my father. I am grateful for my parent's guidance, the establishment of a strong work ethic before me, and their continuous love through the years. Additionally, for introducing me to Christ and being faithful supporters of my ministry. I recall the words of my Dad, "Son nothing in life will ever occur that has not already happened in the Bible, so open the Book." To that end, these timeless words have threaded the fabric of my life with determination and uninterrupted resilience. Moreover, I extend my warmest expressions to my siblings: Kerry Chambers, Darrell McGee and Kimberly Graham.

Subsequently, I offer my fondest remembrance of a wonderful mother-in-law, the late Mrs. Roner Mae Davis for her contagious laughter, caring personality and loving support. I am thankful for "Mrs. Ron," as I fondly called her, for allowing me to hear her personal story of resilience as a young mother with the responsibility of rearing four children after the tragic loss of her late husband, the late Matt Davis.

I honor greatly from the depths of my heart my grandmother- the late Bertha Turner for her pearls of wisdom, resilience in motion, examples of kindness and commitment to God and my grandfather - the late Elmo Turner. Finally, I offer special acknowledgement of my grandparents: the late "Lige" Chambers and Katherine Chambers (my Biological father-Willie Chambers) for giving me lessons from the farm.

SYNOPSIS

There are several ways to cultivate and inspire resilience in people. A good start is finding a practice that resonates with you. It empowers you and motivates you. Now when you're disappointed, it's natural to hunger peace in your heart. You need to be encouraged, you need different results at work, and you need peace in your family. Or maybe you need your financial difficulties to go away.

You have to be careful not to immerse yourself in self-pity for too long. Partaking in feelings of discouragement will nourish the sinful passions of your flesh, and they would become an idol in your life if you chose to turn inward to your feelings instead of developing and strengthening your faith in God.

When you become more resilient, the ability

to overcome adversity comes more quickly. Resilience often indicates the crucial difference between how you handle pressure or lose your cool. There is tremendous power in being resilient, persistent, and determined. And all of it can be learned.

But how do you develop, acquire, or intensify such qualities? How do you become more resilient? In what way can you somehow disregard the challenges in life, persevere, and after all, be successful? This book is about learning resiliency through the P.A.G.E.S. – Prayer, Affirmation, Gratitude, Exhalation, Silence. Nina's story and more in the book can be a source of insight in meeting-up with everyday needs.

At first, you have to realize that resilient people tend to keep a more positive attitude and cope with pressure more efficiently. Individuals with great resilience are genuinely happy people but often have not such perfect lives. Their success and general happiness are frequently credited to their outlooks and habits, which they have cultivated.

CHAPTER ONE

Prayers

Prayer turns the foul odor of despair into the spring fragrance of deliverance. When you find yourself in a situation where it seems the solution is taking one's life, prayer can be the ultimate way. Communication with God is paramount at this time because he is all ears.

Nothing happens outside of prayer. It may not have been your prayer, but somebody else's prayer that has brought you to where you are today. There's no possibility where there is no prayer. Many lives have been changed as a result of someone's prayer. Prayer has since the history of humanity been one of the most potent methods to bring about results.

CHAPTER TWO

Affirmation

Don't be pushed by the fears in your mind. Instead of worrying about what you can't control, shift your energy to what you can create. Emily's life has been about searching. She believes humankind is very powerful than we know. In our day to day life, we must make sure the words of our mouth are aligned with the word of God.

CHAPTER THREE

Gratitude

In all situations and negative circumstances, we ought to show gratitude as it is a sign of strength. A man, by name Mike, showed a depth of power in gratitude. Even when the wife was in intensive care of the hospital, he still appreciated her condition at the moment.

CHAPTER FOUR

Exhalation

Spending a few quiet moments when you wake up and focus on how you are breathing is a simple yet powerful tool you can use to support your desire to wake up, alert, and positively engage with your day, not minding how demanding the day is going to be.

CHAPTER FIVE

Silence

Sometimes, what you need to do is maintain and relate in silence. Silence can solve problems if you know how to listen and keep an open mind. As the master of a ship, Jack often end up giving specific instructions to his juniors; however, in the end, he leaves an open question: "Any suggestion from your end?" This is when he listens, and his juniors were able to give him more insights, and the problem was attended to. Words only can't always do it, but words could.

If you are feeling stuck but want to get your bounce back, remember resilience is about behavior and mindset, which implies you can cultivate it.

TABLE OF
CONTENTS

1. Dedication 3
2. SYNOPSIS..5
3. Building Resiliency.....................................11
4. Prayer, A Tool Of Resilience......................22
5. Use Yourself Talk to Create What You Want –
AFFIRMATION 43
6. Let Gratitude Be Your Attitude Of Choice! 56
7. Inhale and Exhale 70
8. Silence..76
9. PERSONAL RESILIENCE.........................84
10. Life Worth Living.......................................112
11. REFERENCES...116

CHAPTER ONE

BUILDING RESILIENCY

"Trust in the LORD with all your heart, and do not lean on your understanding. In all your ways acknowledge him, and he will make straight your paths" – Proverbs 3:5-6.

Genuine resilience fosters well-being, an underlying sense of happiness, love, and peace. Everyone needs resilience because one thing is certain; life includes adversities.

Resilience is a gift of nature. Like teeny seeds with potent power to push through tough ground and become giant trees, we hold innate reserves of unimaginable strength. Although we can't control struggles we unexpectedly face, we do possess a quality that helps us back to our dreams when the storm is over.

Now when you're disappointed, it's natural to hunger peace in your heart. You need to be encouraged, you need different results at work, and you need peace in your family. Or maybe you need your financial difficulties to go away.

There's nothing wrong with needing things to be different. You have to be careful not to immerse in self-pity for too long. Partaking in feelings of discouragement will nourish the sinful passions of your flesh – 1 pet. 2:11, and they would become an idol in your life if you chose to turn inward to your feelings instead of developing and strengthening your faith in God.

Joseph – son of Israel (Jacob), a young man of seventeen. He can be thought of as a comeback king. Joseph was tending flocks with his brothers, the sons of Bilhah and the sons of Zilpah, his father's wives, and he brought their father a bad report about them.

Israel loved Joseph more than any of his other sons because he had been born to him in his old age, and he made a richly ornamented robe for him. When his brothers saw that their father loved him more than any of them, they hated him and couldn't speak a kind word to him.

Joseph had a dream, and when he told it to his brothers, they hated him the more. His brothers planned to kill him because of jealousy over a prized garment, but they eventually sold him into slavery in Egypt. As the story is told in the book of Genesis, Joseph worked for a man who placed him in jail in Egypt because of a lie – Genesis 39:14-18.

The LORD was with him; he showed him kindness and granted him favor even in prison. During this time, joseph continued his dream interpretation and interpreted dreams for other convicts – resilience. His condition didn't discourage him from expressing his talent. The talent he possesses leads to the ruler who was having dreams about a coming famine in the kingdom.

After interpreting the dream correctly, Joseph

was given a position of great influence. He managed the agricultural efforts of Egypt, and he was in charge of distributing food. Joseph's brothers finally approached him after he ascended to his post. Ten years have passed, and joseph's brothers needed food. He told them who he was, and joseph forgave them for what they had done for years earlier. His brothers and father move finally to Egypt to be with Joseph.

Joseph's story teaches us to recognize we can't determine what the future may hold. Unforeseen circumstances and conditions make up our existence, including calamities and victories.

Life can knock us down flat. It's our measure of resilience that determines whether or not we'll keep dreaming and reaching for our dreams.

A balanced life for a Christian is a life in harmony with God's will, knowing that the one who has created us will always answer and revive us when in trouble (Psalms 86:7, 138:7), and that we can do all things through Him who strengthens us (Philippians 4:13). A balanced individual or community of individuals trusting in the same divine source of strength and striving toward the same moral purpose is the mooring of organization, institution, and system resilience.

Nina's husband died in 2015. He was forty-eight, and they'd been together for seventeen years. It's corny, but he was her best friend—everything in her life revolved around the two of them.

George died from a pulmonary embolism, a blood clot in his lung. It was entirely out of the blue. The kids and Nina were at the beach, and George was back at the house. When he called 911, he couldn't breathe. He was trying to tell the EMTs to call Nina, but he couldn't get the words out. She never saw him alive again.

In the days following George's death, she would leave the house to call friends and family. She didn't want her sons to see her upset. But her eight-year-old son would run out to hug her and hand her tissues. To this day, if she sniffles, her sons ask, "Are you okay, Mom?" she sometimes cries in front of them now because she thinks it's important they know that she is sad too. It's okay to be worried.

From day one, she has consciously talked about George with her kids. She'll often say, "Who does that remind you of?" the boys will reply, "Daddy." she wants to make sure George stays alive in their memories.

On the anniversary of George's death, she took the boys to the ocean. They wrote messages for George on rocks they collected and pitched them into the waves. The things the boys wrote were really precious. It was a special moment together for all of them.

How has she survived? Well, you wouldn't say for sure. She has to keep going for the kids, but more than that, she's sustained by the thought that she mustn't let George down. She doesn't want to disappoint George. She wants to live up to the vision that they had for the kids.

What has helped her the most has been connecting with other widows. When she hears their stories, she thought, "I'm not the only one." Knowing the fact that there is more to life and God has also given her more resilience – the LORD of hosts is with us; the God of Jacob is our fortress (Psalm 46:7).

Some widows may have moved on and gotten married, but they're still wounded. You may find happiness again, but you're never going to be whole. Right now, it's still hard to imagine finding joy for herself, but for the time being, she has found meaning through creating happiness for her sons.

Think of a time when you've had to cope with a situation that you had little control over. Think about what you went through. And look at where you are now. Did you show high resilience and character? Absolutely. Were you even aware of how strong you were and how you showed great character? Probably not, but you still did. Or, if you're in the middle of a bad time at the moment, you're building resilience right now.

There are numerous factors that can help you build your resilience. A crucial aspect is having a great source of role models who can provide the love and encouragement you need to become a stronger person. You also need to have a positive outlook on life and an optimistic view of yourself. You need to be confident in your own strengths and abilities. You also need to be emotionally resilient by being able to understand and cope with very strong emotions and not react on impulse.

Of all of our sources of resilience, spiritual resilience, it is the only one that is self-replenishing. It is proven that the very act in believing adds to our resilience. Like emotional resilience, spiritual resilience grows when shared. But unlike all other resilience, it is spiritual resilience that refills itself.

Husband Convicted

Lilian was sitting in a police interrogation room, her whole world crashed down as she listened to two detectives tell her that her husband had coordinated and carried out the murder of his father.

The words that she was hearing were getting caught somewhere between her ears and mind, and she had trouble even understanding the whole stuff. Learning that the man she had planned life and family with could do such a horrible thing buried her head, her heart, and her hope for the future in darkness. Newly wedded at twenty years old and pregnant, her young adult life and everything she trusted about it were gone.

As much as she wanted to move forward and back into the light, reminders of that day and darkness were inescapable for the next several years. Sunday paper headlines and evening news stories about her husband's case were a regular occurrence. Sometimes journalists would take pity and leave her name out of the print. Other times they would not. Lilian's hometown community whispered, friends walked away, this was a difficult situation for her in her condition.

The husband's trial and sentencing to twenty-two years to life brought even more coverage and chatter.

But in that time of darkness, her beautiful child was born. Even though things weren't the way it was planned, Lilian desire to move forward into a pressing need. And she began to see she had options for her life, and her daughter's life, other than those that were crushed. She would find another option and it would be another dimension for them.

Finding the option was a process that wasn't easy. It required her to step out of complacency and into actions. As she navigated the divorce process, she had to use her voice in a new and assertive way, something that was not usual for her.

Being strapped with all of the financial obligation in the divorce and fighting finance companies over debts he incurred tested her negotiation skills. She faced and dealt with overwhelming emotional fallout of fear, loss of trust, anxiety, and betrayal. She had to hold tight to the people that were helping her move forward and supporting her even if they didn't totally agree with her. Also, she had to set boundaries and even let go of some relationship that get her stuck. For the first time, Lilian was truly choosing to happen to life, rather letting life happen to her. She was choosing to be resilient.

Moving forward wasn't easily 'open'

There were moments when Lilian had to simply rely on will-do attitude rather than a can-do attitude. Self-doubt and defensiveness challenged her. At times, she wanted to sink back under what felt like the new weight of the world. But as she took accountability and responsibility for shaping her future, and that of her daughter, she began to see every place where she had choice in what life would become. She decided that her life would be a life victory, and not of victim of her husband's actions.

In the years since, she has found a healthy and loving relationship with her husband of twenty five years. She has raised three daughters to be strong and independent women. She returned to college at age thirty-five and earned her college degree on the same day that of my oldest daughter earned hers. Lilian has travelled the world. Her experiences have helped her to empower other women to move forward.

Along the journey, resiliency muscles have certainly been tested. The moment that changed everything has lasting impact. Emotions, questions, anger, confusion, and hurt didn't just disappear when she chose something different for their lives. But as issues arise, she feel, address, and work through them. She learned from them and moved forward.

But as issues arise, she feel, address, and work through them. She learned from them and moved forward. How was she able to attain such feat?

P. – PRAYERS

A. – AFFIRMATION

G. – GRATITUDE

E. – EXHALING

S. – SILENCE

"The human capacity for burden is like bamboo – far more flexible than you'd ever believe at first glance." – Jodi Picoult.

CHAPTER TWO

PRAYER, A TOOL OF RESILIENCE

When you see yourself moving into unexpected turbulence, select PRAYER on the instrument panel because it automatically connects you to the heavens control tower to guide you through the darkest hour of your life – Dr. Michael Chambers.

Prayer is the oldest form of worship and is universal to all types of religions and believers.

Even atheists rely on prayer in some way or another to make it from day to day. Man has always marveled at how things happen in life and how to change those things that have not yet happened. The answer for the Christian has always been a prayer to God, Jehovah, in the name of His son Jesus.

Prayer turns the foul odor of despair into the spring fragrance of deliverance – Dr. Michael A. Chambers. Nothing happens outside of prayer. It may not have been your prayer, but somebody else's prayer that has brought you to where you are today. Prayer is the prerequisite of possibility. There is no possibility where there is no prayer. Many lives have been changed as a result of an answered prayer. One can only imagine the billions of lives that have been changed as a result of someone's prayer. Imagine, if you will, how many prayers are offered up every second, every minute, and every hour of every day. That's a lot of prayers and a lot of impacted lives.

Prayer has since the history of humanity been one of the most potent methods to bring about results. Prayers come in different degrees of intensity and definition. A 'desperate prayer' to save a life, perhaps yours or someone else's, is one type of request. Prayer can also be a simple 'prayer of gratitude.

HARRIET TUBMAN – SARAH HOPKINS BRADFORD'S BIOGRAPHY OF HARRIET TUBMAN.

Harriet Ross Tubman was christened Araminta when she was born in 1822 to slave parents on a plantation in Dorchester County, Maryland. Her ownership was transferred to the stepson of her original owner, who moved her with many of her family to his own farm in Bucktown. She was often hired temporarily to masters, who were brutal and neglectful. Many of the other members of her family were illegally sold, thus breaking up the unit. She was once nearly killed by something thrown by an angry overseer that struck her head. As a result, she suffered narcoleptic seizures and sleeping sickness for the rest of her life.

She was now serving another master, Edward Brodess, in 1849, who needed to sell slaves to cover his debts. On hearing rumors that she and her brothers were going to be sold – **Sarah Hopkins Bradford's biography of Harriet Tubman.** She began praying that her master changes his mind "I prayed all night long for my master till the first of March." When her prayers did not work, she changed her prayer to "Oh Lord, if you ain't never going to change that man's heart, kill him, Lord, and take him out of the way."

A week later, Edward Brodess died. Harriet felt guilty and full remorse. The death of her master brought more uncertainty over her and her brothers' futures. She had already seen three of her sisters sold, and she was not going to let the same happen to them.

Although the brothers had a second thought, she resolved to escape, even if she was caught. It was a better option than being sold to the south. Harriet was ready. She had saved enough money hiring her labor and knew people who conducted the Underground Railroad. She firmly believed that God would guide her. Harriet traveled at night so that slave catchers would not see her. Just as other fugitives, she followed the North Star that guided her North. The first person who saw her was a white woman who was a Quaker; she sheltered her for the first night and gave her instructions on what to do next. With the Quaker's instructions, she executed the escape. The Quaker, whose name is unknown, was a member of the Underground Railroad network that provided safe houses and transportations for fugitive slaves.

Over the years, Harriet Tubman repeatedly returned to the eastern shore mainland, rescuing other slaves, including her brothers, Henry, Ben, and Robert, their wives and some of their children.

"I'm going to hold steady on you, and you've got to see me through "

Above ejaculation was recited regularly by Harriet Tubman when she led runaway slaves to freedom. The nineteenth-century "Moses," having been enslaved, never lost a person along the Underground Railroad and attributed her successes to her deep belief in God. She would say this prayer just as she began to engineer one of her daring escapes.

ELIJAH

Elijah was an Old Testament prophet of God. He did many wondrous works for God, some of which made him popular among people; other times, he was less than popular. But he knew that whether his deeds were popular or not, he must obey God's commands. But just as Elijah listened to God's voice, God himself listened to Elijah. Their relationship was one that in the Old Testament was reserved for priests and prophets, but today is available to anyone who accepts

Jesus into their life.

In these verses from 1 Kings, Elijah had been staying with a widow woman and her son. He had already blessed the widow and proven himself as a man of God by miraculously causing her food not to run out, so that the widow, her son, and Elijah could all eat during a time of famine and drought. But during his stay, the widow's son became ill and died. When Elijah prayed for the child's life to return to him, God answered right away. This is a dramatic, immediate instance of God answering prayer.

PRAYER WITH FAITH

Most of all, our prayer must be coupled with faith. Faith is the substance of things hoped for, the evidence of the things not seen (Hebrews 11:1). Without faith there is no possibility in prayer. Prayer without faith is just empty conversation, and wasted time, breath, and effort. The Bible teaches us that all things are possible. Christians love to quote that verse, but often fail to complete the statement. The point of the possibility is for those who would only believe (Mark 9:23). Circumstances and situations can usher in doubt, and doubt can accompany itself with our prayer. But prayer refuses to travel any place with doubt as its passenger. As powerful as prayer is, it is no match for doubt. Doubt renders the most elegant, thought out, and sincere prayer impotent. Uncertainty always brings fear, along with it. Fear continuously deactivates possibility.

How do we know when we have caused there to be no possibilities in prayer? Look closely and examine your prayers. Root out the fear in your life. You will find fear dressed up as laziness, or fear dressed up as procrastination, or as excuses, and the list goes on. How prepared are you for an answered prayer? Here are some factors to consider: Have you considered who can benefit from your prayer other than you? Is your prayer in the will of God? And, finally - Do you believe in the possibilities in prayer?

"The tongue has the power of life and death, and those who love it will eat its fruit" – proverb 18:21. In our day to day life, we must make sure the words of our mouth are aligned with the word of God. Some negative confessions may block the blessings that the Lord has already appointed for us. We eat the fruit of what we say, so if we want to be blessed, we should speak blessings into our lives.

IMPORTANCE OF PRAYER

We used to struggle in our prayer life. We would feel guilty, condemn ourselves and even evade the topic of prayer with other saints because we felt like a failure. Some people thought that their good work, faithful church attendance and tithing would offset the fact that their prayer life wasn't what it should be for someone like them that have professed an undying faith in Jesus. They would try to have devotions before they pray and fall asleep while reading the scripture. They engage in corporate prayer at church, but that didn't satisfy the intimacy they needed with the Lord that comes through personal, private prayer.

Prayer is one of three powerful tools we have as believers. The other two tools of fasting and studying the word are only complemented by having a strong, consistent prayer life. The bible says in the book of James 5:16 it states "The effectual fervent prayer of a righteous man availeth much." This declaration that James makes reminds us that God hears and responds to prayer. He loves when we seek Him, worship Him and acknowledge Him. He loves to bless us! He wants us to know Him in a personal way. Prayer offers us that. Prayer gives us a calming peace and security that only the Father can provide for us. This peace that surpasses all understanding that is mentioned in Philippians 4:7 is given to us freely by a God who loves us unconditionally.

The role of prayers in securing and maintaining your peace cannot be over-emphasized. A life without prayers is one full of troubles and that will soon be terminated. A praycrful person knows better not to play with his prayer time since experience has taught him that he rules over the devil on his knees. This book emphasizes the importance of prayer in maintaining your peace of mind.

HAVE YOU REALLY PRAYED ABOUT THAT DIFFICULT SITUATION

Prayer is a religious practice seeking to activate volitional connection to our most high God. You can either choose to have an individual prayer or a communal prayer. The reason why we pray is because our Lord Jesus Christ directed us to do everything in prayer trusting that it shall be done. "And pray in the Spirit on all occasions with all kinds of prayers and requests. With this in mind, be alert and always keep on praying for all the saints" (Ephesians 6:18). There are very any other verses of the Holy Bible where Jesus talks about prayers.

To some, prayer is the only way to give them confidence, to pursue a very difficult task. To others, prayers are one way to keep their hearts light and to feel that closeness to God. Christians have learnt the importance of frequent praying, and starting from morning prayers, lunch prayers, dinner prayers and other prayers are some of the much known prayers. Online prayer is one of the most widely spreading ways of praying since one doesn't have to move to the local church. You can have your prayer request while at home or at your place of work.

Jesus gave his disciples a model prayer when

they requested him to teach them how to pray. You and I often say these words as our own prayer. Jesus also gave them a model for prayer, sort of a "thumb-nail" sketch of the content and attitude of prayer. When you pray, these words can serve as a guide. They are probably very familiar to you. It seems a little obvious, but the prayer reminds us that, when you pray, pray to God. God is intimate and holy, our divine and heavenly parent. To hallow God's name means that we keep a reverent attitude with regard to the ultimate reality the name God represents.

The request your kingdom come is a plea for God's ways and will to become the reality of this world and of our lives. Give us daily bread points to being aware of the needs in us and around us, and have the ability to distinguish needs from wants. Forgiveness is a two-way street. Being forgiven by God doesn't depend on our forgiving others because we can't earn God's love. Our forgiving others, however, indicates awareness of having been forgiven - that there is in us a core of grace. And regarding the time of trial or temptation, God don't bring us there. Keep us from falling away. Give us the ability to hang on and hang in, to find ways to believe and trust.

Beyond this, then, how should we pray? Do you notice something curious in Jesus' prayer? Almost every statement is imperative, like a command. Hallowed be your name! Kingdom, come! Give daily bread! Forgive our sin! Don't bring us to trial! It's almost as though we are ordering God!

We live in a world full of need - for healing, for justice, for meaning, for truth, for food and medicine, for inclusion and for love. As we allow ourselves to become aware of these overwhelming needs, they move through our minds and hearts. They are impossible for us to fix. All we can do is send them all to God in prayer. And we let them go, trusting God to be God. And God sends back to each of us the particular dimension of need and possibility that exactly corresponds to our unique identity and giftedness - the need that's got our name on it.

How we pray, our ability and talent in prayer, is not a factor in prayer's effectiveness. It doesn't really matter whether or not we use the right words or that we're good enough or spiritual enough. What is vital is that we do pray. Any amount of faith that we bring to prayer is enough for God to use. God's nature, God's power, and God's faithfulness are all that matters in whatever space we open.

What about those other images Jesus used? If there's a friend who doesn't want to help you. With persistence on your part, he will help, but God is more faithful. So be persistent in prayer. Keep asking. Keep seeking. Keep knocking and doors will open. When a child asks for food, some may give snakes or scorpions, but God is much more faithful. God always gives the Holy

Spirit. The Spirit always brings healing, calmness and wholeness. It's not our ability or piety that makes prayer effective, but rather our willingness to pray. What really matters is God being God-like.

For nothing is impossible with God – Luke 1:37. God is able to do just what he said he would do, He's going to fulfil every promise to you. Don't give up on him, he's never going to give up on you. All you need do is seek Him, and do the right thing always and He will make your way smooth!

TYPES OF PRAYER

Without question, for the sincere Christian, prayer is extremely important as it develops a personal relationship with our Creator God. But, in prayer, can a Christian ask for the wrong things? And just how do we know the correct way to pray? What lessons might Jesus, God's beloved son, teach us where prayer is concerned?

For Christians, prayer is simply communication between our Creator God and His created beings, His children. As we go through the scriptures we see that Jesus often prayed that God's perfect will be done in His life. The same should be so with us! With each passing day the need for our Father's guidance, strength and wisdom becomes ever the more important.

Let's look at the different forms of prayer

- Agreement Prayer

This type of prayer involves more than one person coming together to render their common supplication to God. We are introduced to the prayer of agreement in Matt. 18:19 when Jesus said, "Again I say to you that if two of you agree on earth concerning anything that they ask, it will be done for them by my Father in Heaven."

To effectively use the prayer of agreement one must be sure that all involved with this prayer must be in complete agreement. When anyone asks another to pray in agreement with them concerning a matter it is extremely important that all parties concerned understand the specifics of the prayer request. And if anyone does not feel they cannot honestly join in any kind of prayer of agreement he/she should not allow themselves to become a part of such agreement.

- Prayer of Faith

Count the number of times in Holy Writ when Jesus said to someone, "According to your faith." Reference to peoples' faith is constant. Even though it was His power that healed them, He always credited their faith with being the catalyst. In fact, when Jesus went to His hometown, we are told, in Matt. 13:58, that He did not do many mighty works there because of their unbelief. Certainly Jesus did not suddenly lose His power on that visit to Nazareth. It clearly was contingent upon their belief, the same as it is today!

Mark 11:24 is recognized to be the key verse for the prayer of faith in which Jesus says, "Therefore I say to you, whatever things you ask when you pray, believe that you receive them, and you will have them."

Of great importance is the fact that Mark 11:24 does not say when you will actually see the result of your prayer. Nor does it say how long it will take for one's prayer request to become a reality or manifest.

This is where many Christians become discouraged and even distracted in their own prayer beliefs. We must always remember that God lives in one eternal now. There is no past or present for Him. But we are temporal beings who live in the context of time.

So when we pray in faith or trust, God immediately gives us what we have prayed for. However, He gives it to us in the spirit realm. When He chooses to give us the answer in the natural world, due to a number of factors, it may take time for the answer to manifest itself.

Many times we are looking for answers in the natural world before we look into the spirit realm. We become impatient for answers. This is often the time(s) when the enemy of our soul(s) start(s) working on his infamous tactics of steal, kill and destroy.

We must never forget that God answers prayers, and He will answer each one of our specific prayer requests in line with His Word. However, it is our faith, our trust that brings His answer to us, out of the spiritual world and into our personal physical world. His power never changed. So what changed? It was the people's level of faith, their trust, mixed with His power.

A powerful, yet simple spiritual explanation for this is the fact that God will not do something against our personal will. God will not, He cannot, violate anyone's free will. So if anyone doesn't have faith, or if they are not able to trust Him to do something, He won't arbitrarily override that lack of faith and/or trust.

- Praise and Worship

"Worship the LORD with gladness; come before Him with joyful songs. Know that the LORD is God. It is He who made us, and we are His; we are His people, the sheep of His pasture. Enter His gates with thanksgiving and His courts with praise; give thanks to Him and praise His name" – psalm 100 vs 1-4.

In this type of prayer, you are not asking God to do or to give you something. This prayer type does not ask God for any kind of direction nor is it dedicating your life to God. Instead you are just praising the Lord, thanking Him for His bountiful blessings and mercy which He promises that are renewed every day. You are telling

Him how much you love Him.

Luke 2:20 is a wonderful example of the shepherds glorifying and praising God for all the things they had heard and seen, and also describes their reaction when they saw baby Jesus.

Luke 18:43 gives an example of prayers of thanksgiving in the story of the blind man glorifying God when he was healed. All the people who witnessed this miracle also gave God praises.

In Luke 11:2 Jesus gives specific instruction concerning the infamous Lord's prayer when He told His disciples how to pray by saying, "When you pray, say, 'Our Father in Heaven, hallowed be Your name.'"

John 11:41 Jesus gives yet another wonderful prayer example when He said, "Father, I thank You that You have heard Me," when He referred to His prayer regarding Lazarus.

In Phil. 4:6 we are admonished in a prayer example given by Paul when he wrote to the Philippians, saying, "Be anxious for nothing, but in everything by prayer and supplication, with thanksgiving, let your requests be made known to God."

- Dedication and Consecration

The prayer of dedication and consecration works when there are at least two Godly alternatives available and you may not be getting clear direction concerning the one that God wants you to take. When one's direction is unclear, yet all options do appear to be right and legitimate, this would be the perfect time to say, "I am going to go with this option, Lord. I want it to be your perfect (not permissive) will. Now please show me if I am making a mistake here." Trust me, if you are in error, He will show you!

An outlined prayer of dedication and consecration is found in Luke 22:41-42. Here Jesus withdraws from James, Peter and John and kneels down and prayed, saying, "Father, if it is Your will, take this cup away from Me. Nevertheless, not my will, but Yours be done."

Jesus was actually saying, "If there is any other way to do this, (then) let's do it that way." The great learning point here for all of us is the fact that Jesus is flexible when He asks the Father to show His (perfect) will by saying, "Nevertheless, not My will, but Yours, be done."

Without question when one is not absolutely certain which direction should be taken in any decision it is absolutely correct, even "Godly" to ask for confirmation!

- Intercessory Prayer

Intercession is simply praying in behalf of someone else. A person may be incapable of praying for him/herself. Such would be the case if someone is extremely ill, on drugs, demonically possessed or perhaps mentally impaired. Also it may involve praying for such things as the government, the church or specific prayers based on the knowledge of someone's personal needs.

In Ephesians 1:15-18 Paul makes it clear that he is interceding in prayer for the church at Ephesus when he wrote, "Therefore I also, after I heard of your faith in the Lord Jesus and your love for all the saints, do not cease to give thanks for you, making mention of you in my prayers; that the God of our Lord Jesus Christ, the Father of Glory, may give to you the Spirit of Wisdom and Revelation in the knowledge of Him, the eyes of your understanding being enlightened; that you may know what is the hope of His calling, what are the riches of the Glory of His inheritance in the saints."

It is important to note here that Paul does not set himself in specific agreement with anyone. This fact makes this particular prayer an excellent example of Intercessory Prayer.

Another good example of Intercessory Prayer is found in Paul's greeting to the Philippians that is found in Phil, 1:3-4 when he wrote, "I thank my God upon every remembrance of you, always in every prayer of mine making request for you all with joy."

- Binding and Loosing

Like all things in God's system the prayer of

binding and losing only works in line with God's Word and His laws which is clearly set forth in Matt. 18:18-19 when Jesus tells us, "Assuredly, I say to you, whatever you bind on earth will be bound in Heaven, and whatever you loose on earth will be loosed in Heaven. Again I say to you that if two of you agree on earth concerning anything that they ask, it will be done for them by my Father in Heaven."

One is able and has authority to bind foul spirits that are at work in people's lives. Also, one can loose angelic spirits to work on their personal behalf in those areas where God has already promised results. When one prays in this manner, God affirms it, in Heaven, and puts His seal of approval on it. Binding and losing must be based on the authority God has granted His children in Scripture, not on some (whimsical) desire.

God has provided each type of prayer for a specific purpose. Though you may use more than one at any given time, it is important to be clear about which type you are using and why, and to be aware of its limitations. If you follow the examples in the Bible, you'll be sure to use them properly.

Clearly we see, as set forth in the above examples that our prayers, whether they are prayers of supplication, faith or trust, should all be mixed with praise and worship.

WHY SHOULD WE PRAY

Prayer is the power of a connectedness with God that can change the world. Prayer affects the life of the one who prays. Your prayer opens a space in your life for the Spirit to move to transform the world, to transform individual lives, and to transform us. We help bring the Kingdom of God from invisible to visible reality. It happens little by little through individual people of faith.

The Christian faith tradition believes that God respects human initiative and the free exercise of human will. This means that God acts only when we open the space. Praying, then, is inseparable from doing and doing is inseparable from praying. The results of praying are growth and transformation. For individuals, praying brings transformation and spiritual growth. For humanity, prayer brings social transformation and reform.

Prayer is life beyond our understanding. It is a miraculous connection. Prayer is action, a mystical channel through which God touches and transforms the world. When you pray, first listen and then speak in words that reveal themselves through the open channel of your life. The Spirit moves through you and into you and there is prayer. God's kingdom comes in you and through you, and prayer continues, and God's will is done.

CHAPTER THREE

USE YOURSELF TALK TO CREATE WHAT YOU WANT – AFFIRMATION

"The tongue has the power of life and death, and those who love it will eat its fruit" – proverb 18:21. In our day to day life, we must make sure the words of our mouth are aligned with the word of God. Some negative confessions may block the blessings that the Lord has already appointed for us. We eat the fruit of what we say, so if we want to be blessed, we should speak blessings into our lives.

All you need do is say it and believe it, and God will perfect it for His glory. God's people can trust God to change their tomorrow. God isn't leaving His people out to dry like a sheep among wolves. HE is intricately involved in creating a new future – "for I know the plans I have for you" declares the Lord, "plans to prosper you and not to harm you, plans to give you hope and future" (Jeremiah 29:11).

GOD'S WORD

God's Word is alive and full of power. Rightly applied, it can change any life. His Word is the truth, eternal truth. And He has given us His Word so that we may live thereby. One of the ways we can apply God's Word to our situations and circumstances is by speaking His Word on a consistent and daily basis.

The principle of speaking, confessing, and affirming God's Word is life-transforming. Death and life are in the power of the tongue, and when we fill our mouths with His Word, we are positioning ourselves to receive the results His Word promises. Through affirming His Word, we are declaring that His truth is greater than any fact which may presently exist in our lives. His Word can overcome, change, and alter any circumstance and bring us victory. By affirming His Word daily, we can walk free from negative habits, sickness, hurt, and fears. He created the heavens and the earth through His Word. He caused things to be through His Word. And His Word still has life-changing power today.

Here are statements you can make daily, affirming God's Word. Spoken consistently, morning and evening, His Word will improve the conditions of your life more and more:

- Colossians 2:9-10
- "I've been made complete in Christ."
- If you're feeling that void in you that you can't achieve a particular goal, speak it until confidence is built.

Philippians 4:1

- "I can do all things through Christ, who strengthens me."
- This is excellent to affirm if you have problems with self-confidence and find yourself being fearful of taking action. Affirm this truth daily until confidence rises within you to do things you thought you could not do.

2 Timothy 1:7

- "For God hath not given us the spirit of fear, but of power and of love and of a sound mind."
- Affirm this twice or three times daily to relieve yourself of timidity and a fearful spirit. Speak it until boldness rises within.

Isaiah 41:10

- "Fear thou not, for I am with thee; be not dismayed, for I am thy God. I will help thee; yea, I will strengthen thee; yea, I will uphold thee with the right hand of my righteousness."
- If you are facing loneliness and depression, affirm this passage from God's Word daily. It will minister His peace to your soul.

Colossians 3:1

- "Since then, you've been raised with Christ, set your hearts on things above, where Christ is seated at the right hand of God."

1 Thessalonians 1:4

- God loves me and has chosen me

Begin affirming God's Word today.

THE TRUE PURPOSE OF AN AFFIRMATION

"Man often becomes what he believes in himself to be. If I keep on saying to myself that I cannot do a certain thing, it is possible that I may end up really becoming incapable of doing it. On the contrary, if I have the belief that I can do it, I shall surely acquire the capacity to do it even if I may not have it at the beginning" – Mahatma Gandhi.

"The picture that we have ourselves – our self-concept will always determine how we respond to life" – Myles Munroe.

Believe it or not, the words in an affirmation have no power to change anything in your life. As I said, affirmations are not magical incantations, and you may be surprised to learn that the purpose of an affirmation is NOT to change anything outside of yourself.

Yes, your ultimate goal is to create better circumstances in one or more areas of your life, but that's not the first thing that needs to happen. Instead, the true purpose of an affirmation is to change the way you FEEL about a given topic. When you feel differently about something, you will start to think and believe differently about it. And when you think, feel, and believe differently, you will take different actions - and therefore, you will change the results you receive.

LOSING WEIGHT

Emily's life has been about searching. She always knew there was something we had forgotten about living this life on earth. She believes humankind is way powerful than we know.

Emily had been dieting ever since her teen years. She is now in her fifties. Now, when she diet, nothing happens at all, no matter how long she restricts her food intake. However, she can easily gain 5 pounds in a matter of days, just eating like an average person

She decided to infiltrate her thinking with a thought about losing weight. After all, she figured she had nothing to lose, as diets weren't working anymore.

So, the first thing she did was deciding never to diet again. That was a significant portion of why her affirmation worked. She believes that the unconscious thinks you are going famine when you diet. Therefore, it eventually wants to hold onto your stored fat for the next famine that may come along. It also makes you gain back any fat you've lost. It doesn't consider the good or bad of losing weight.

She had just recently gained 8 pounds. Her statement was short and straightforward, "I'm ------ pounds"; it was 8 pounds lighter than her current weight. She said it, especially when going to sleep at night, over and over, and when she woke up in the morning. But, she also repeated it throughout the day and if she woke up at night.

She weighed after two weeks, and nothing had happened. She weighed again after three weeks, and the 8 pounds was gone.

The second she tried this, she went 10 pounds lighter. She kept up the repetitions for two months, but there was no weight loss. So, she thought it was just a fluke. But, she decided to try it again with only five pounds less. She lost 5 pounds, but it took a full month.

Again, she tried it with 5 pounds. This time she had the opportunity to say the affirmation much more than she had in the past. It took only five days this time.

The exciting thing is that she eats whatever she wants. She had neither gained nor lost a pound. Her unconscious believes that she weighs the last amount she affirmed to it, no matter what. Or, at least until she convinces it further.

CHOOSING YOUR AFFIRMATION

Shakti Gawain, the author of Creative Visualization, offers the following advice for choosing your affirmations:

- Always phrase your affirmations in the present tense, as if it already exists. Say, "I enjoy being at my ideal weight" instead of saying, "I will reach my ideal weight."
- Affirm what you want, not what you don't want. Instead of saying, "I am no longer a procrastinator," say, "I always get things done on time."
- Don't simply go through your affirmations by rote; add positive feelings and emotions to your affirmations.
- Choose affirmations that feel right for you. If you come across an affirmation that you like, but you would feel more comfortable changing a couple of words, go right ahead.

Affirmations are simply statements that we make to ourselves; it's our self-talk. You use affirmations all the time, whether you're doing so intentionally or unintentionally. If you make a mistake and you think to yourself, "I'm always making mistakes, I never do anything right," you've just made a negative affirmation. If instead you make a mistake and you think to yourself, "That's OK, I can correct this," you've just made a positive affirmation.

Your self-talk has an enormous impact on your conscious and subconscious minds. By repeating positive affirmations, you can reprogram your thought patterns. Creating new thought patterns will allow you to begin to change your underlying beliefs and the way that you think and feel about yourself, others, and your place in the world. In this way, you can improve your life dramatically through the use of daily positive affirmations.

HELP WITH AFFIRMATION

Although the use of affirmations includes repeating them often so that our subconscious will take over, there is nothing "otherworldly" about them. We are simply training ourselves to think positive.

Do affirmations help? Yes. Most definitely! Here is how to choose affirmations that will help you make your life better.

- Make Your Affirmation Believable

If you don't believe your affirmation is possible, you won't be able to put effort into seeing it happen. For example, "I will marry a millionaire," is so far from our current life that we can't find it believable. It is a dream, not an affirmation.

An affirmation should state what you want without being too much of an exaggeration. A much better declaration would be: "I will marry someone whom I love and who makes a comfortable living." This affirmation is one that you can believe and can take steps to achieve.

- Repeat It Often

For your subconscious to pick it up and make it automatic, it has to be repeated often. Basically, you are programming your mind to remember what you want so that you subconsciously make decisions that will help you achieve your goal.

One way to repeat affirmations is to put them on post-its that you place around your house (on the fridge, on the bathroom mirror, on the cupboard, and other places you'll see them). This can be effective on its own or can be used with other affirmation techniques.

- Don't Try To Control What Happens

While you should take steps to achieve your affirmation, don't try to control what happens in your life. If your affirmation was to marry someone who makes a comfortable living, and someone comes into your life who makes minimum wage, the decision is yours. You can choose to let go of your affirmation or to continue looking.

How can it be used?

- Affirmations can be used to create a positive attitude
- Affirmations can be used to create good habits or to replace bad habits with good ones
- Affirmations can help a person to achieve their goals

- Affirmations can help maintain a calm or balanced manner in the face of a threat or provocation
- Affirmations can help change your life

I feed my *spirit*.
I train my *body*.
I focus my *mind*.
It's my *time*.

Effectively, affirmations need to be stated in positive terms. They also need to be stated in the present tense. Affirmations tend to be a statement of belief; they work on a subconscious level and work on the principle of a self-fulfilling belief. Therefore, the more you say or recite the affirmation, the stronger the message becomes, and the more the message is accepted by the mind of the person reciting the affirmation.

Each of us has an 'inner voice,' a form of 'self-talk,' that we use in thinking or talking to ourselves. Many of us may be unaware of this; it is most evident when we have time to ourselves to think or if we have the opportunity to rehearse a speech or presentation we have to give. Affirmations utilize this self-talk to communicate their message to us. All too often, for many of us, our self-talk is negative, we use it to tell us when we have made mistakes, or to put ourselves down, to criticize ourselves, or to say that we cannot/ should not do something. Affirmations turn this around and get us to use positive language to develop or reinforce positive messages to ourselves.

Traditionally, affirmations have been written or spoken, sometimes both, yet affirmations are also linked to learning styles. Many of us tend to think more in images rather than words; others think or learn better through actions or sounds. The fact that affirmations have tended to be seen as a written or spoken method, may account for why many people have not yet fully seen the benefits of affirmations; written or spoken affirmations do not fit easily with the preferred learning style of those people.

Affirmations, of course, need not be words alone; they can be visual or involve movement or gestures. In this way, affirmations can be used successfully by a wide range of people. Indeed, many of the best uses of affirmations have tended to employ more than one method of communicating the message. So an affirmation may link a positive statement with an image. In this way, the user sees associates the positive message with the image and vice-versa. Similarly, an affirmation can be linked to a gesture, such as clicking a finger, so then the person can perform the gesture and recall the message.

CHAPTER FOUR

LET GRATITUDE BE YOUR ATTITUDE OF CHOICE!

"Naked I came from my mother's womb, and naked shall I return there. The LORD gave, and the LORD has taken away; Blessed be the name of the LORD."

Job had lost everything – his children, wealth, and health. His friends gave up on him, and his wife offered no support. Job felt as though his life was over; the only option was death. But as Job says, even if God did 'slay' him, he would still trust and never give up on God. Still, Job found the need to be grateful and uttered the above statement – an expression of faith and thanksgiving. That's resilience, and being grateful not minding the sufferings can go a long way.

Job is a wealthy man living with his family in the land of UZ. God brags about Job's goodness, but Satan argues that Job is only good because God has blessed him abundantly. Satan challenges God that, if given permission to punish Job, he (Job) will turn and curse God. That's where the pains and sufferings of Job started.

In one day, Job receives four messages, each bearing separate news that his livestock, servants, servants, and ten children have all died due to marauding invaders – natural catastrophes. Job tears his clothes and shaves his head in mourning, but he still blesses God in prayers. He said: 'Naked I came from my mother's womb, and naked shall I return there. The LORD gave, and the LORD has taken away; blessed be the name of the LORD' – Job 1:21.

Satan, upset by Job's attitude towards God, took Permission from God again to do more harm. This time, Job was afflicted with horrible sores on the skin. He couldn't eat or sit or do anything; it was a severe pain all over. His wife advised him to curse God and die, but Job was resilient.

At first, Job's friends try to help Job, but they quickly turn to accuse him of some sort of hidden or known sin. Job knows that this is not the reason and tries to justify himself against their accusations. But his justification quickly turns to self-righteousness, and that is a sin before God. Job's friends say, *"Is not your wickedness great? Are not your sins endless? You demanded security from your brothers for no reason; you stripped men of their clothing, leaving them naked. You gave no water to the weary, and you withheld food from the hungry, though you were a powerful man, owning land– an honored man, living on it. And you sent widows away empty-handed and broke the strength of the fatherless. That is why snares are all around you, why sudden peril terrifies you"* (Job 22:5-10). This brings God's righteous indignation upon Job's friends (Job 42:7-17).

After all the pains, Job was restored by God. He ended up much better off than he was in the beginning. He had considerably more than when he began his suffering, and even though God did not answer Job 'why' he was allowed to suffer so terribly, in the end, Job had more blessings than any man on the face of the earth at that time. The application for Christians today is that God will bless those who endure to the end and that someday, God will reward us with unbelievable blessings that cannot compare with what we have today (Rom 8:18, 28). We all shall pass through pain in this life. It is appointed to humankind to suffer. It is a fallen world. We may not know the "why" today, but someday we probably will. Instead of asking "why," we should ask "what." What is God up to? What is God trying to do in me? The "why" will have to wait for someday in eternity. Until then, we cannot fully grasp the purpose of God, but we know that He will not allow us to suffer into eternity. One important thing is that Satan

could not lay a finger on Job, nor can he on us.
God will not allow this (Job 1:12. I John 4:4).

GRATITUDE AND PEACE

While there are many ways to bring peace
into your life, living a life filled with gratitude
has to be the quickest. One cannot be angry and
grateful at the same time. It is hard, or maybe
impossible, for anyone to feel gratitude and any
'negative' emotion or thought at the same time.
Try it yourself and see what results come from
being grateful and trying to get angry; make it
real, though, don't try to fake anger or gratitude.

For example, you are driving to/from work
in the 'usual' traffic snarl that you are so used
to. Then, unexpectedly everything comes to a
screeching halt, and you sit. Minutes go by, and
nothing moves; you keep checking the time and
strain to see what the traffic is about. Then frustration turns to anger and blame sets in, resulting in complaints to anyone who will listen. If
you are alone, you complain just to feed your
anger, because your usual drive to/from work
was interrupted.

Since we get trapped in our habitual way of living, believing this is the way things are, we have
little time to express gratitude for anything.
We may think we are grateful for something in
our lives that we take for granted but never express gratitude verbally or mindfully. It is like
the groom that tells his bride, "I love you. If that

ever changes, I'll let you know", then never says the words to her again. Expressing gratitude is huge.

There are two times during your day when the verbal expression of gratitude creates the best results - when you wake up, and before you go to sleep. Expressing gratitude first thing in the morning sets the pace for your day. I used to sit on my deck with a cup of coffee in the morning and give thanks for everything I could think of - the new day, the sun, the clouds, birds, sounds, quiet, my family, and so on. It worked well until I noticed that there was a gap between getting out of bed and the gratitude time, sometimes filled with negativity.

When I changed to giving thanks upon getting out of bed, my day lightened up. It is like the old saying about how you feel when you look in the mirror in the morning saying either "thank you God it's morning" versus "oh my God, it's morning." You want your day to start off with a smile versus a frown, don't you? Doesn't a smiling face look better in the mirror than a frowning face?

Gratitude lifts you as you begin your day. Wearing a smile while you drive to work, or wherever, and expressing gratitude raises your vibration. And it's likely to keep it there. If you run out of things to feel grateful for, makc something up. For example, if, at the moment, you have expressed gratitude for everything you can think of, then give thanks for something you want in your life that you don't presently have. This is actually a way to begin a manifestation.

Starting the day with gratitude sets the tone or vibration of your mind and lifts your attitude. If during the day, something comes along, and it will pull down your vibration, expressing gratitude will offset the lower vibration if that is necessary. It may be that you need to feel the lower vibration for some reason, but that is again, beyond the subject being discussed here.

Ending your day with gratitude is likely to help you get to sleep faster and lay the groundwork for a more restful sleep. It also helps put behind you things that occurred that you need not remember or deal with anyway. Some situations seem to hang around and bug us all night, even though they had little meaning, to begin with. After a while, you will be able to discern when briefly reviewing your day, what situations are worth remembering, and which ones are not.

GRATITUDE, A SETUP FOR FAILURE

An attitude of gratitude has always been a precursor for living in good moral standing. Those that are not grateful, we are told, will be miserable, will not go the heaven, or will not receive more. But this very notion that we must be grateful to "get" something else is a set up for failure. Here is why.

To be truly grateful for something means that

we value it, appreciate it, and have an authentic unconditional love of it. Gratitude, as a platitude, is actually the exact opposite of truthfully appreciating something or valuing it. Feigning gratitude in words or even with forced emotion is another form of lying. If you are grateful, you live within it; you do not need to advertise it. Not that there is anything wrong with promoting it, but unfortunately, many think a demonstration of gratitude is merely convincing ourselves and others how much we have it.

We have been told, "Be grateful for what you have or else you will not receive more." So, we started ticking off our items to be grateful for and making sure that everyone else knows it too. We are also told that we must be thankful for God. Those that are not grateful to God are in big trouble in the hereafter. We are also told that "not" being grateful is the behavior of only the vilest, selfish people.

We shout and reverberate our gratitude for God because deep down, we fear that not being grateful means we will not have a chance for His grace or worse that we might go to hell. But if we are not truly thankful for what we have, it's not because we are bad or evil, it's because we are asleep (metaphorically). Gratitude is an innate quality to the soul and individual spirit of man. We don't have to feign it; we are it. If we experience moments in our lives that point out our un-gratefulness, we should be shouting hallelujah; I have been shown the light.

Here is an example. Most people feel that they should be grateful for their jobs. Many people today have been heard to say, "I know times are tough, so I am so grateful for my job." Which is another way of saying, "I really hate my job, but at least, thankfully, I am better off than a lot of other people right now." This is not gratitude, it's resignation and attempt to build up our self-worth from the backs of other more unfortunate unemployed people. First of all, if you were genuinely grateful for your job, you probably would not feel a need to declare it. You would live it! Your job would be an extension of your gratitude for it. You would know this because your job makes you feel good, helps you to contribute, and provides not only monetary needs but emotional and spiritual desires as well.

If you are complaining about "it," whatever or whoever "it" is - news flash, you are not grateful. If you cannot be happy within this moment, and you are constantly looking forward to the next day, or the next exciting event, or even wishing this moment would hurry up and be over, guess what, you are not grateful for what you have. When you wish for, pine for, fight for, anything, you are not grateful for what you have. If you see anything as missing from your life, then you are not grateful for it. Gratitude is an unconditional acceptance of what IS. Seem harsh?

Some of you might say, "Hey, I wish for, and I

will fight for peace." Why? Is it missing in your life? If it wasn't, why would you feel like you need to fight for it? For others? Find it in your own heart first, then see what needs to be done to promote peace. Peace, Love, Joy, and so on are not won because we refuse to accept their absence - they are won when we admit their presence. See, if we can't embrace the wholeness and completeness of where we are now, then we will always be grasping for it in the future.

No amount of demonstrating, shouting, commiserating, or scheming will change it, even if we do it with the banner of love and gratitude in our hand. Peace is. Love is. Gratitude is.

The resolutions to what you are "not" truly grateful for cannot come from an attitude of denial. Don't feel bad because you still resent Aunt Mary for what she said ten Thanksgivings ago, feel curious. Not for why Aunt Mary said it, but for why you still resent her for it. What wake-up call is this giving you? When you value Aunt Mary, when you appreciate her and show that appreciation in your actions and behaviors towards her - then you are grateful for her. Until then, work on the real root cause of the conflict in you. This does not mean you have to be fake or unkind to Aunt Mary just that you know in your own heart and soul you still have feelings of conflict about her that YOU need to address.

The notion that we cannot have more until we are grateful for what we have is true, but the part that was left out was, you must TRULY be grateful for them. That is again, the setup. The idea is that if we "act" grateful (and some of us even truly believe we are grateful by the English definition of the word), then more things will work out our way. Then we scratch our heads in wonder about why things are not working out for us; we are so grateful after all! Acting ungrateful by not recognizing or being flowery with our thanks and so on, will obviously make others not like us (we are told anyway). But really, acting ungrateful is just being honest. That does not make it admirable, perhaps, but neither is fake gratitude.

Altruist behaviors that are done out of disingenuous gratitude require recognition. If you expect recognition or are disappointed because you didn't get it, then your grateful actions are not genuine. These types of generous actions are done for your benefit, not the recipients. This is not to say stop doing them - they still may be helping someone else, but please consider your motives and your intentions when giving to others to express your gratitude. Don't worry, if you are truly grateful, you'll show it appropriately. It will be natural and effortless. You do not have to come up with elaborate or flamboyant action to demonstrate true gratitude.

We have things and people in our life that we are truly grateful for. You may have noticed that when you just let gratitude unfold from genuine appreciation and value, these things just continue to grow and take root in your life. Take some time to consider how you value yourself and others. Be an advocate to others by expressing gratitude for yourself and to God by how you conduct your life. If you are not there yet, don't fake it. Be patient and compassionate instead. Yes, gratitude is an essential element for living from the highest moral and spiritual standpoint, but so are honesty, authenticity, and love. Gratitude, like other inherent qualities you always have available to you (love, joy, peace) are not fake it until you make it emotions. It takes awakening to see it in yourself, not enforcement. Expressing unconditional honesty and love IS gratitude. You should almost NEVER have to say it. It must be lived.

GRATEFULNESS IS HEAVEN ITSELF

Gratitude is a signature strength that can be tested and measured. It is an appreciation of someone else's character. It is one of the most endorsed strengths around the world. Gratitude shows a strength of character that contributes to life fulfillment and satisfaction. It implies awareness and thankfulness. Appreciation can be built by focusing on positive aspects.

The famous stress researcher, Hans Selye, claims that two attitudes more than any other influence the quality of everyday life. And on these two emotions "depend our peace of mind, our feelings of security or insecurity, fulfillment or frustration, in short, the extent to which we can make a successful life. The most destructive emotion is revenge. But in contrast, among all the emotions, there is one which, more than any other, accounts for the absence or presence of stress in human relations, that is the feeling of gratitude.

Mike Mcadams visited his wife Cheryl in the intensive care unit of the hospital. How is she? An anxious friend asked as he exited her unit. Mike replied. "She recognized me; we prayed together and held hands. And then we quoted the passage about thanksgiving in the book of James that says, consider it joy, my brethren when you face trials of many kinds. "You know," he added, "it's impossible to be anxious and thankful at the same time."

Is there an area of your life you would like to improve? Try pouring gratitude into it and notice what happens. Make a daily commitment to speak and write and breathe about what is good in this area you want to improve. Do your gratitude experiment for a month and notice for yourself what happens.

CHAPTER FIVE

INHALE AND EXHALE

Meditation is surrender. It is not a demand. It is not forcing existence your way. It is relaxing in the way life wants you to be. It is let-go.

With life events out of our control, knowing how to control our breathing to build resilience and restoration through our nervous system is a tool required to respond rather than react to these times.

When many people think of meditation, they think of some bald guy sitting in a candlelit temple with his legs crossed in a way that no average mortal could ever twist or bend (and possibly hovering while doing all of the above). Well, the truth is, there are many forms of meditation - all the way from the flying zen master technique above to a much simpler and more practical approach to release stress without worrying about floating away.

The key to meditation merely is slowing your heart rate and allowing your mind to focus on your breathing and nothing else.

Have you ever woken up feeling slightly "off-balance," anxious and worried about something?

Maybe you are mourning the loss of a loved one and wake up feeling empty and alone. Perhaps you have recently separated from your partner and lie in bed and ponder what your future holds. You may be aware of rumors at work of possible redundancies and are fearful of what will happen to you and your family if you are made redundant. No matter what your particular issue is, you wake up, feeling heavy-hearted, grumpy, tense, and "don't feel right."

Have you noticed that when you wake up and feel like this, things just don't seem to flow, for example, you don't have time or energy to prepare a nutritious breakfast and make do with a handful of biscuits or packet of crisps as you rush out of the door; maybe you argue with your children about the untidy pile of clothes and books on their bedroom floor or the copy of the report you thought you left in a safe place, is no longer there and you feel your head beginning to throb as you panic as you try to remember where it could be.

During these moments, it is elementary to wish you could hide, return to bed, and curl up with a good book!

If you can identify with the above scenarios, have you ever thought "there must be a better way to start my day" and wondered what you could do to try and set your day off on a better footing.

Spending a few quiet moments when you wake up and focus on how you are breathing is a simple yet powerful tool you can use to support your desire to wake up, alert and positively engage with your day.

Learning how to breathe correctly is an essential part of life. The slower and deeper you can breathe, the more you allow oxygen to enter and flow through your body. This expands your lung capacity, stimulates, and opens up your heart, which has an instant effect of making you feel brighter and happier.

INHALE.
EXHALE.
REPEAT.

Next time you wake up and feel out of sorts, off-balance, or plain tired from lack of sleep, try this simple Yogic Breathing Exercise to energize, rebalance, and align your energy.

- Lie on your back in your bed, with your eyes closed. Stretch out your legs (about 12-18 inches apart). Tuck your chin slightly into your chest, stretching out the back of your neck. Make sure you feel comfortable.

- Rest the palm of your right hand firmly yet gently on top of your navel and your left hand just below your collar bone.
- Take a slow, steady breathe in through your nose from your abdomen (right hand) and breathe slowly up to your left hand.
- Slowly breathe out.

Repeat the lines below three times during the deep breathing;

- Inhale: Our Father which art in heaven,
- Exhale: Hallowed be thy name.
- Inhale: Thy kingdom come,
- Exhale: Thy will be done in earth, as it is in heaven
- Inhale: Give us this day our daily bread
- Exhale: And forgive us our debts, as we forgive our debtors
- Inhale: And lead us not into temptation
- Exhale: But deliver us from evil:
- Inhale: For thine is the kingdom,
- Exhale: And the power, and the glory, forever, Amen.
- Breathe slowly and deeply this way for rounds as you feel your mind become calmer and quieter.
- Slowly release your hands, gently stretch your body, rest awhile in your bed and enjoy the calm and peace you have now created in your body.

Relax and Have a Good Day!

CHAPTER SIX

SILENCE

There's "A time to keep silent, and a time to speak" – Ecclesiastes 3:7. Being quiet can be a struggle, but it can also be a good virtue to have. The scriptures commend those who can keep the peace and listen, however, discourages being quiet due to timidness. Through God's words, we can be empowered to speak out, for it can lead to great things.

Solitude is the creation of open space in our lives by purposely abstaining from interaction with other human beings, so that, freed from competing loyalties, God can find us. Solitude is one of the most important disciplines for the spiritual life.

It's for being alone with God. Solitude is completed by silence. There's much to be said about solitude, but what's most important is that it is a way to do nothing. Yes, do nothing. Don't try to be productive - even in bible study! Solitude and silence are an opportunity to focus on your intimacy with Jesus, in times of difficulties. Not only when in pains, but in times of joy and plenty as well.

Unhook from your daily responsibilities and the people you interact with, to attend to the Lord alone. In solitude, you don't try to make anything happen. You bring your naked self to the Lord to be with him.

Not every situation in life requires advice or direction. Some situations need your silence for them to be resolved. This silence allows the mind and thought the process to reach the places that you desire it to and seek the answers that have more meaning as opposed to if they came verbally. Typical scenarios where silence speaks volumes and gets you the solutions that you desire;

RELATIONSHIPS

For a good relationship to exist between two people, whether it is husband and wife, parent and child, friends or colleagues, requires a certain level of understanding from both sides. When difficult issues arise, both sides should have their say, but then there must come a period of silence when both sides must listen to the other and their thoughts. This is when silence speaks volumes. This silence allows you to hear what you won't normally do if you were too busy making your point heard. This silence will enable you to analyze the situation and see the reason for your feelings and those of the other person. Without this silence, it would be difficult to reach some compromise or understanding because you would be too busy preserving your own needs.

AS A WEAPON

Silence can also be used as a weapon when you are faced with difficult situations. No one can fight someone who isn't willing to respond to ridicule or abuse. It is a very effective way of defending yourself in times of trouble, and even the strongest of minds are put to the test by your silence. The thing to remember with this usage of silence is whether you do so in the righteous or unrighteous manner. What you sow is what you reap. If you use this to defend yourself righteously, then it shall be effective. If in an unrighteous manner, then the consequences can be dire. For example, if you are hiding something that could save another, you must speak up. Your silence, in this case, is unrighteous. On the other hand, if you keep silent to prevent conflict or argument, then you are using this righteously.

SOLVE PROBLEMS

It's not all. Silence can solve problems in several additional ways in the professional world. If you are facing an interview board and you are completely charged up and ready to answer every question, be silent, listen intently, and understand the question first. Your answers will sound professional, and the board will be impressed by poise and grip because you took the time to listen and really think out the words that you say.

If your friend is instructing you over something routine that you have done a number of times and you don't need instructions, do not be impatient, just listen. You might find a piece of new information and new ways to approach the same task!

'Listen to silence; it has much to say.' Silence can solve problems if you know how to listen and keep an open mind. As the master of the ship, Jack often end up giving specific instructions to his juniors. In the end, however, he leaves an open question. He asks: "Any suggestion from your end?"

This is when he listens intently and wait for new information. You would be surprised at all the ways his juniors have surprised him with their insights and innovative ways to do things. This is how silence can solve problems that are far from anything words can do by themselves.

SILENCE IS GOLDEN

We have long since forgotten that the world "screams" while our souls "whisper." With noise, all else is drowned out, but with silence comes the sound of our heart when it speaks.

As Richard Mahler states, author of Stillness: Daily Gifts of Solitude, Simplicity, and Silence, ***"Silence allows us to open the door to our unconscious mind, feel the yearnings of our heart, follow the wisdom of our intuition, probe the origin of our aversions and understand the truth of our experience."*** Speaking of silence, he goes on to say, ***"We, at last, get in touch with our deepest secrets, strongest passions, fondest wishes, and happiest memories."***

Sometimes silence is a sign of fear or oppression, or as a way of withholding the truth, or when choosing not to speak out against great injustice. That is not the silence of which Mr. Mahler speaks, but instead, he refers to the golden silence that takes us away from our fast-paced, noisy lives and transports us to a beautiful place where we can heal and grow strong once more. It would be wise for more of us to "mine for that gold" as it will lead us on a path to a sacred place, free from worry and fear.

Without these moments of silence, we are doomed to keep on moving and searching, all the while, allowing what is good and worthwhile to remain a step behind. If we spend all of our time talking about what we think we know, then we will never hear anything new or important.

American historian James Truslow Adams wrote, *"Perhaps it would be a good idea, fantastic as it sounds, to muffle every telephone, halt every motor, stop all activity someday to give people a chance to ponder for a few moments on what life is all about, why they are living and what they really want."*

Understanding the need for silence is one thing; knowing how to reclaim it is quite another. The first step is in understanding that time spent in silence is not wasted time or loss of productivity. The reality is that silence is its own reward because it is in silence that we can re-connect with our inner voice and rediscover our sense of time, well-being, happiness, and ease.

Committing to some moments of silence each day does not necessarily mean we have to carve out new time within the already busy day to fit them in. They are already there waiting! All we have to do is turn off the TV, radio, or cell phone in order to tap into our beautiful silence.

It really isn't that difficult to add silence into our lives, and here are just a few ways to do so:

- Take 5 minutes a day to meditate. That's all the time it takes to reap the benefits of the most recommended, powerful practice of silence.
- Go for a walk without the aid of earphones. Leave the music behind. Listen to your thoughts.
- Turn off the TV during your morning coffee and just BE.
- Take a few extra minutes in the shower and experience the relaxing water on your body.
- Start to engage in hobbies and pastimes that require no type of sounds, such as reading, writing, and knitting.
- Choose to work in silence when you are performing a task with another. Gardening and other physical activities are where this seems to work best.

Make time for silence in your life. Give silence

a place in each day. Celebrate the fact that silence is a piece of your ultimate being. Its subtle,
intricate role in your life will bring moments of
celebration and joy.

CHAPTER SEVEN

PERSONAL RESILIENCE

Resilience fuels perseverance, which accelerates the journey to success. A substantial level of resilience rests in the core values you believe in, but most important, it is acting on and living a life reflective of those core values. Working on your core values promotes every other characteristic of success, including integrity, personal honesty, accountability, self-respect, attitude, professionalism, humility, and empathy, to name a few. A saying attributed to the Chinese Philosopher Chuang Tzu states, "Heaven is internal, humanity external, and virtue comes from the heavenly. Know heaven and humanity's actions; root yourself in heaven and follow virtue. Then you can bend, stretch, rush forward, or hold back because you will always return to the core and it will be said you have achieved the supreme."

Recognizing the interdependency of the many principles of success resulting from your resiliency will provide you with a blueprint for self-understanding and achievement. You are the architect of your life's design and the construction manager of its progress. The rewards for being resilient include learning from the struggle, adding a new life experience, reflecting with a different perspective, and gaining a greater appreciation for what you have.

The birth of resilient behavior stems from our upbringing and the parental and environmental influences we experienced. It is widely accepted that growing up around resilient individuals strengthens a person's resiliency. Most important, we all can be resilient by practicing the core values we believe in. It is bouncing back from failure and disappointment that puts the spring in our step because it provides self-confidence to carry on. Personal resilience is all about the following;

- Social Involvement
- Emotion Management
- Personal Mission and Values
- Alignment to the workplace
- Problem Solving Approach
- Physical Wellbeing
- Concentration and Focus

SOCIAL INVOLVEMENT

"Let your light so shine before men, that they may see your good works and glorify your Father in heaven" – Mathew 5:16.

"Pursue peace with all people, and holiness, without which no one will see the Lord" – Hebrews 12:14

Social involvement is essential to build resilience. There's no need to view social participation as not being fair as a Christian. As a Christian, social involvement is necessary for your growth. Not only to mingle with believers but as well with unbelievers so you can impact their lives and may transform them for better. Note it may take time, but at the end may be worth the stress. You have to view life from their point so that max transformation could be attained in a short period. There's a need for social involvement!

To achieve a high level of joy and happiness in life, we must be socially involved with people. This involves getting along well with others, having friends and companions, and offering help to those who need it. We are all part of a social environment, and our social environment provides us with many opportunities for fun, excitement, enjoyment, charity, and love. Indeed, one of the most rewarding things you can do is to reach out to others to connect with others on a deep level.

Involvement with others, however, can also bring pain. You can experience hurt feelings, anger, character attacks, job loss, sadness, and loneliness. But you can use your Conquering Force to maximize the rewards and minimize the frustrations and pain. Achieving success in the social area of your life is the art of learning to interact with others and care about them-and their needs-while they care for you- and your needs. When you have social success, you experience a sense of inner peace and happiness. You gain an incredible sense of value while discovering how rewarding it is to be a caring and giving person.

When people are asked what being social means to them, they often respond that it means getting together with friends more frequently or making new friends-often, including attending parties and other fun-filled events. The more socially skilled people will also mention such things as being involved in the PTA or service organizations like the Lions Club or Rotary International. But there is more much more.

Being meaningfully involved with other people provides a veritable banquet of wonderful heart-to-heart experiences. The social area of one's life can also become financially profitable for him/her. In one instance, as a direct result of being involved socially, a friend brought in more than a million dollars to his company.

If you are not already a social individual, it's encouraging you become one very quickly. You should enjoy and be enjoyed; love and be loved.

Doing this is quite easy once you have the formula for social success, and it will help you enjoy greater success in other areas-ultimately influencing how fast you adjust to trauma, how much you earn, the services you receive, or render, where you live, and with whom you work.

If you are seen as a great person to work with or be around, you tend to receive better service, earn more money, get promoted faster, and in general, get along better. You don't need to allow the problem you have at the moment to weigh you down. It is crucial that you learn the social skills that can make you right as a person. It can be as easy as trying to improve the life experience of those who struggle by showing them a better way to be-by word and example. If they aren't receptive, move on.

Everyone knows people who are challenging to be around. They are negative, pessimistic, easily angered, or arrogant. They whine, complain, and blame. These are the people who are not open to change or growth. Because they are unwilling to progress emotionally or socially, they stay stuck and don't enjoy life.

Loneliness and solitude are not just anti-social; they can have adverse effects on your health and even result in a shorter life expectancy. Fortunately, there are plenty of opportunities out there for seniors looking for ways to get involved, make friends, and create social engagements.

Even if you don't consider yourself a social butterfly, you may want to begin increasing your amount of socializing as you get older. Social relationships and engagement with others have been clinically shown to help the elderly age more gracefully as well as encourage better health over time.

EMOTIONAL MANAGEMENT

"A hot-tempered man stirs up strife, but he who is slow to anger quiets contention" – Proverbs 15:18.

"Do not be anxious about anything, but in everything by prayer and supplication with thanksgiving, let your requests be made known to God. And the peace of God, which surpasses all understanding, will guard your hearts and minds in Christ Jesus" – Philippians 4:6-7.

"Have I not commanded you? Be strong and courageous. Do not be frightened, and do not be dismayed, for the Lord your God is with you wherever you go" – Joshua 1:9.

The challenges we encounter daily are enough to give us emotional trauma that we tend to lose focus and not considering God in what we do. Even as Christians, we may lose guard and begin to question God and our existence. These things (problems) are bound to manifest not minding our background, but are you ready to face them, even as unbelievers?

Managing emotions is an arduous task for some but a skill that is essential for personal relationships. We all have and experience emotions, whether we like it or not. Managing emotions mainly deals with unpleasant emotions: anger, fear, frustration, depression, despair. Emotions are the feelings we experience day to day, such as happiness, pride, boredom, sadness, anger, and frustration. Emotions are a part of our everyday existence as they move through the body, affecting our state-of-mind, performance, health, and energy. Emotions cannot be helped. Emotions we don't even realize we are feeling can influence our thoughts and behaviors; they can also travel from person to person like a virus. Due to this virus-like state, it is of the most utmost importance for those in positions to influence not only their own emotions but understand the need to monitor and perhaps influence the moods of others.

One of the hardest things to learn when it comes to working with the law of attraction is how to manage our emotions. This is such an important skill if you are to attract the things that you want into your life that you should devote some time and energy to it. We attract to us what we think and feel about the most, so the more we let our negative emotions rule, the more negative things we will draw to ourselves. Sometimes it can be not very easy to stay positive when the world around us throws the stuff at us it does, however, regardless of what the world does, we need to manage our emotional state.

Every day we all have to deal with people or situations or things in our lives that cause us to feel down and out or angry or any number of other negative emotions. That is a normal part of life. The difference is in how you allow it to affect you. Any number of things could happen from a failed relationship to failed friendships, trouble, and stress on the job. Your ability to keep your eye on your goals and manage your emotions and keep them in the positive realm is directly in alignment with your success and your ability to attract everything you want in your life.

There are some things you can do to keep your emotions in a positive state. First, you need to keep your mind on where you are going regardless of what happens right now. Right now is only a temporary situation, but your goals and the future you want to build become a part of your everyday life. A runner doesn't focus on the pain in his legs or the people next to him. He keeps his eye on the finish line and pushes with everything he has until he crosses that line. Then he can look back at the pain and the other runners and what happened as all of that is a part of the past at that point, and as we all know, the past is gone and will never return.

Another important thing to remember when things happen is that this one thing isn't your entire life. If you have someone at work who gives you problems, remember that that person is just that person. It isn't your spouse, or the hobbies you have, or all of the other things you have going on in your life. The goodwill always outweighs the bad if you remember to think about them. There is always better going on in your life if you take the time to see it. We often allow what is happening right now to cloud our entire emotional state and life. We allow things to consume our thinking, and this will only slow down your progress and accomplishments.

Remember to manage your emotions, or your feelings will control you. Keep your eye on the goal and keep moving toward it no matter what. Even if things do get so bad that it feels as though nothing but bullets and bombs are flying at you, keep moving. Keep your eye on the prize. Even with death one step behind you, keep moving. Manage your emotions and keep them in the positive, and as soon as you begin to recognize that they are moving into the negative, make a shift in your head and your heart. The universe rewards those who take action and manage their life.

What About Your Health As Regards Emotional Management? Another area affected by developing Emotional Intelligence skills is health. Negative emotions fuel higher cortisol levels often called "the stress hormone. Excessive cortisol levels, over time, can cause acid reflux, sleeplessness, asthma, ulcers, loss of bone mass and osteoporosis, low sperm count, redistribution of fat to the waist and hips, and fat buildup in the arteries, which can lead to heart disease and numerous other diseases (Mc-Craty, Borrios-Choplin et al. "The Impact of a New Emotional Self-Management Program on Stress, Emotions, Heart Rate Variability, DHEA and Cortisol" Integrative Physiological and Behavioral Science 33(2):151-70, 1998). Mismanaged emotions, correlated with dysrhythmias in our Autonomic Nervous System, are associated with many diseases, including asthma, chronic fatigue, depression, hypoglycemia, hypertension, and many more. Learning to transform from negative emotions into positive productive ones throughout the day or night over a sustained period of time has been shown to have a positive impact on many health-related problems. In many programs, participants most frequently mention a significant elimination or reduction of sleeplessness, often in a couple of weeks.

Developing Emotional Intelligence skills is not difficult. People have realized the benefits in a very short period by applying simple, proven techniques consistently. They have reported improvements in all of the categories - decision-making, relationships, and health.

PERSONAL MISSION AND VALUES

Clarity of purpose and direction is one of the keys to career and life success. To develop your personal clarity of purpose, you need to do three things. First, define what success means to you. Second, create a vivid mental image of you as a success. Third, clarify your values. Once you identify what success means to you personally, I suggest that you develop a clear mental picture of you as a success. This image should be as vivid as you can make it.

This isn't always easy to discover. If you're young and still trying to figure out your mission, don't worry. It takes time. That's why I always tell people to be open to new ideas and thoughts, as you never know what you might pick up.

Your mission comes from deep inside you and is unlikely to change over the long run. Some persons had lots of different jobs in lots of companies and have been self-employed for over 20 years. Through all the change, one thing has remained constant -- their desire and passion for helping others and making sure that those around them felt their impact, even their employers. In their heart of hearts, they know that they are on this earth to help others navigate the ambiguities of life to reach their goals. However, some persons may not have a likely mission.

Unlike your mission, your vision will change over the course of your life and career. This vision fits into your mission, but it had a specific short term time frame. Your vision needs to be consistent with your mission. However, unlike your mission, your vision should change as you grow and develop in your career and endeavor.

So, where does all this leave us when it comes to thinking about the clarity of purpose and direction? Here's how I suggest you think about it.

Your purpose is your mission -- your reason for living, your passion, what you are on this earth to do, something that is unlikely to change over the long run.

Your direction is your vision -- short and medium-term goals that define the course you will take your life and career.

The common-sense point here is simple. Successful people define the clarity of purpose and direction for their lives and careers. Your clarity of purpose and direction should include both a personal mission (your purpose) and a personal vision (your direction). Your mission is your reason for living, why you are on this earth. It is unlikely to change over the long run. Your vision is a short or medium-term goal that defines the direction you will take over the next three to five years. It will change are you grow and develop in your life and career. Your vision must be consistent with your mission. As stated earlier, your mission is not easy to find; it takes patience and commitment; this helps to stir once resilience when found because it's a force on its own.

ALIGNMENT TO THE WORKPLACE

Unless we work as a priest or anyone connected to religion, then our day to day jobs very rarely have a mention of our faith. It is a taboo to mention faith and even worse to mention Christianity. This pressure makes us believe that we have to leave this part of us at home before we adorn the attire of our workplace. Below are examples of how we can practice our faith at work while balancing the demands of the work environment.

- Loving Your Neighbor As Yourself

This is the second most important commandment, and we must all uphold this at work. Loving your neighbor as yourself means overlooking certain aspects such as the need for revenge and for listening to gossip. People will always challenge us, whether it is to discredit us or to test our faith. People will always talk about us, and if we were honest, then we should know that we also talk about others. If it is right in both cases, then we must be resilient enough to ignore this. Our focus should be on sharing, helping the team succeed, and making sure that we deliver more than is expected. If we want to please God, then we must perform to the highest of our abilities in the job place. It is not our duty to promote the Lord. No one can buy his gifts, and they are not for sale. His work would show through us, and eventually, those who seek our help will ultimately want to know where this help comes from. They would see the light within us and know beyond a shadow of doubt that the Lord works through us. They will confess his name even before we mention it and bow down before him, as he promised. The point here is not to say we should not confess the Lord's name. It is to say that we should give to Caesar what is Caesar's.

- Ambition And Beliefs

Another problem faced by Christians is how to uphold our ambition without becoming over-zealous and forgetting our beliefs. For this, we must also remember that God would not give us something that we can't handle. In scripture, the Lord also says we should not be careful for anything but put it in prayers and supplication. Ambition is one of those things that is difficult to measure during the time of implementation. We cannot see an opportunity and miss out on it because we wanted to be nice. In other words, we saw a chance at scoring and passed this unto someone else. Our gain in life will always be someone else's loss. It is impossible to measure everything to balance. On the other hand, we should not go out of our way to make others suffer while we gain an advantage. We should not take credit for others' work because we are ambitious. However, if we have worked hard, then we deserve what comes our way. As in the bible, the laborer is worthy of his rewards.

- Avoiding False Prophesy

We also must practice tough love in the workplace. This means everybody is rewarded by the Lord according to what he wishes to give them. We should not become false prophets promising things for others that they cannot receive. It is our duty to uphold morals, to push our colleagues to succeed and improve themselves. However, what every man gets in return is what God has intended for him. Riches are not just there for the taking because of hard work; riches are also a responsibility for those that have them and how they use them. Not everyone was meant to have everything because not everyone has a generous heart to give when they have wealth. It is the nature of things. In Christianity, we learn the values of long-suffering, humility, and patience. If we have endured getting to where we are, then these attributes are active within us. This means that we would turn to our faith in wealth or poverty. If we prophesy about wealth, then we should also prophesy about the responsibility that comes with it.

Why do we need to have workplace wellbeing? Because we spend so much time in the workplace, even if your workplace is home, it needs to induce wellbeing and make sure that your work-life balance is suitable for your needs. Many professionals who go out to work will not have the creature comforts around them; if you are» hot desk-ing, outsourced, small office-ing, open planned, Nomad working," or moving from office to office, you know that it is not so easy to get your comforting and familiar things around you. However, there are ways that you can achieve holistic wellbeing in the workplace no matter what your workplace looks like.

One of the issues which you might consider if stress is ruining your life is how to build a structure around you that you can take anywhere you work.

Why would you do this? Well, most organizations are demanding what they now call "Emotional Resilience" in their workers. What is this new concept? Well, with the demand for workers not to be made ill by their work, organizations are stating that their workers need to take responsibility for their resilience to the emotional impact of their job.

From gas fitters to social workers, you will experience stress as unique to you. As an employee, you will, therefore, need to know what impact stress is having on your perception of reality, your thinking, and your behavior

It is not a new concept; its meaning is related to vigor in the workplace and is measured on an individual's ability to complete work because they have the physical, emotional, or cognitive strength to meet the demands of the job.

How will this affect some workers? Well, basically, if you do not know what the test for emotional resilience is, you will not know how to prove it.

So, what ways can you ensure you prepare yourself for things which may affect your well-being at work?

Although there are thought to be three significant ways of ensuring a balanced life, which equally equates to wellbeing in the workplace i.e., spiritual, physical, and emotional wellbeing. You need to establish patterns to keep you on track to ensuring that you are achieving a balance in your life.

There are five key areas that workers may wish to consider in getting them to this balance.

- Awareness of your needs
- Self-Care

How you intend to take care of yourself while you do your job and all available resources which are inside your organization as well as external to your organization need to be mobilized in order to care for you.

1. Career development or goals

Basically, whatever you choose to take on to keep you motivated and stimulated and to achieve your potential both in work and in your own life.

2. A reviewing system which is effective

How you are going to keep yourself on track to achieve the things which you think are important and to ensure you get the right life-work balance, which makes a difference to you.

3. Positive mind frame

And finally being positive about yourself and what you are achieving or have achieved. This is especially important as the shifting of your emotional position at will so that you can affect the desired results for you, enhancing your thinking, and increasing the use of positive behaviors will have major benefits for you.

You do not need to be dependent on what your organization has to offer you alone; you can take some control and obtain emotional resilience and vigor at work while ensuring a healthy balance in your life.

PHYSICAL WELL-BEING

Physical well-being is when our body is well tuned; we eat well, we exercise and we usually maintain our body well. We also can call physical well-being our capacity to control well our capacity to "survive" in the world. We manage our money well and we are able to create the results we want in the world of business.

Mental wellness or well-being means our mind is well balanced. We are able to think clearly and our thoughts are well organized. We see things pretty much the way they are. We are able to think logically through steps that will get us from point A to point B. Our actions are well structured and have a strong reasoning behind them.

During times of stress it is becomes even more necessary to guard your physical and emotional health, because for those of us who are able to help others, our ability to help and stay strong for them becomes even more important.

Besides keeping ourselves fit with physical exercise there are other components affecting our physical well-being. Some of these include:

Diet - It is no secret that we need to feed our body properly to fuel it for the exercise that is vital to balanced physical well-being.

Sleep - It has long been known that the average requirement of sleep per night is 7 to 8 hours. Today, unfortunately the average sleep per night has been reported as 6.7 hours on week-days. Lack of sleep not only causes us to feel all around cruddy moving slower and showing visible signs of sleepiness. We become forgetful, can't concentrate, make bad decisions and are more irritable.

Alcohol - heavy and regular alcohol consumption has been proven to have negative affect on the brain, liver, pancreas and heart. Some reports show that moderate consumption can have a positive effect on the heart. Moderate consumption is identified as 1 drink for women and 2 for men on a daily basis. Greater consumption for a longer period of time can cause brain shrinkage, decreased muscle coordination, learning and memory impairment, high blood pressure, heart disease, stroke and pancreatitis. Mouth and throat cancer have also been associated with heavy, regular alcohol consumption.

Smoking - today, everyone knows that smoking can cause lung cancer and possibly even death. It is written on all the cigarette packs. It is taught in schools. Pamphlets can be found in every Doctor's office. To live better longer we need to be aware of other negative affect that smoking has on our body like:

- Less benefit from physical training
- Less muscle strength and flexibility
- Disturbed sleep patterns
- Shortness of breath (3 times that of non-smokers)

The bad news continues. Effect that smoking has on our bones and joints can increase the risk of osteoporosis, hip fracture, rheumatoid arthritis, low back pain as well as exercise related injury like bursitis, tendonitis sprains and fractures.

Because you want to live to see your grandchildren and be able to enjoy activities with them, you need to use good and natural products to live better longer. In particular multivitamins can serve as a meal replacement to keep you nutritionally balanced.

THE POWER OF RESILIENCE AND HOW TO CULTIVATE IT – A SHORT STORY

Feb 7, 1980 to the late Jimmy T. Sleight and Susan Sleight But, my father passed away when I was of the precious young age of 5, leaving my mom to care and raise my two sisters and I as a single parent. I must say that we were blessed after the death (murder) of my father, my mother was able to purchase us a home in Washington, DC (working class) area. We were able to attend some of the better Washington DC public schools. But unknown to us kids, this was the number one struggle that led to depression and tough times for my mother. As an adult, I now see and understand her struggles. The battle that later led her gambling addiction. An addiction that then caused us to experience our water being shut off, lights turned off, house phone cut off, cars repossessed, and later evictions and the loss of two homes. My mom's addiction and struggles became more visible and apparent to the point where she left us and moved to Philadelphia.

This was also around the time when I started to exhibit behavior concerns. I became a runaway at the age of 11. I started cutting school, fighting, and became very disrespectful to my teachers and surrounding adults to the point where I was permanently suspended from another school in Washington DC. I then transferred to a night school program, where I was placed on probationary status to transition back to day school. Upon completion of my night school requirements, I moved back to the city with my aunt and uncle because, at that point, my mother could no longer tolerate my behaviors (fighting, running away, fighting, stealing, and disrespectful). I was then registered to attend Lake Clifton

High School (Baltimore city) in the 11th grade.

But the severe behaviors ultimately led me to numerous counselor appointments and doctor office visits, until one day a psychiatrist looked at my mother and my mother had poppy eyes and said have you had this child's thyroid checked. I was later taken to see an endocrinologist, and I was diagnosed with Graves Disease, a form of Hyperthyroidism. A disease that causes high-level hyperactivity; no sleep, large appetite, high metabolism, poor hair quality, fast heart rate, dry skin, and more.

Shortly after I was diagnosed and started permanent medical treatment and turning my life around, my mother left me and my two sisters in a rental townhouse, where the lights were cut off by BG&E, and she left us to care for ourselves. I was devastated because, of course, I believed, and my sisters thought my mother left because of me because I was the problem child. Neither one of my sisters caused my mother any problems. Both of them were good kids in school, athletic, and always doing the right things. I, on the other hand, was ugly with big eyes that people ever made fun of, maintained about a 65-70 average, constantly suspended, and had very limited friends. I'm tearing up just at that thought of my childhood life. To remember and think about how I thought and believed I was so ugly. My eyes were so big because of the thyroid condition to the point where they could pop out.

Sometimes I would be the joke of the class.

But, I would assume that my mother made contact with my cousin because, as I vaguely remember, my cousin came to our rescue and moved my sisters and I out of the house the day before our scheduled eviction. But, at that point, my mother was gone with no goodbye. We just woke up one morning after being in the dark (no lights) for several days, and my mother was gone. At that point, we moved with our cousin, who later moved us all into a townhouse to accommodate the needs of her new roommates, my two sisters, and I. I remember this so clearly because this all happened in my senior year of high school and my girlfriend's mother purchased all my senior prom items in order for me to attend the senior prom. All these distresses weren't able to stop us achieve our dreams and goals in life. Look at me now, I know there are many who had gone through the same or more ordeals, still they are able scale through. It's all about Grace, God allowing the resilience in you to work exceedingly. I'm so proud of my sisters and I, it's a wonderful achievement for us.

Dr. Sinclaire currently serves as the Director of Operations for Evergreen University in the Business Continuing Education Division. She has demonstrated exemplary leadership skills in grant compliance, budget management, policy and procedures, marketing, and human capital development and management. She possesses a special attribute which has contributed to her resilient life; she lives a prayerful life, very optimistic and always says some words of affirmation that will lead her for the day, even in her prayers as well. I've been privileged to enjoy her company, and one of the things I admire most is her Grateful heart, she is thankful for everything not minding how little it is.

Sinclaire began her professional management career at Community Services of Maryland, Incorporated as Human Resources Payroll Manager. She later advanced her management career and became a Residential House Manager and later a Personnel/Training Manager. In continuing to advance in her career endeavors, she became an Assistant Director for The Chimes, Incorporated, a domiciliary care unit that housed elderly residents. In that capacity, she was responsible for the total health and welfare of residents and the professional development of staff.

Dr. Sinclaire served in the United States Army Reserves and received an honorable discharge as a Supply Sergeant. In this capacity, she was responsible for maintaining and tracking military supplies. Under the direct supervision of a Master Sergeant, she supervised a platoon of 10-15 soldiers.

She started on her educational professional career path at Evergreen University as a Budget Analyst and then promoted to Coordinator of Contracts and Grants Management. In this position, she maintained and ensured compliance of over $8,850,000 in reimbursable cost grants and $900,000 in flat-rate contracts. She completed and was awarded the Carl D. Perkins grant for over 1 million dollars for two consecutive years. Both years Sinclaire implemented, managed, monitored, and completed federal reporting requirements for each award. She also facilitated grant workshops, where she has demonstrated expertise with federal, state, and local regulations and guidelines.

Furthering, professional academic management, Dr. Sinclaire was appointed to serve as the Director of Operation for Evergreen University, Business and Continuing Education Division. In this position, she demonstrates strong leadership in marketing, advertising, enrollments, retention, partnerships, budgets, grant compliance, partnerships, and an entrepreneurial spirit. She has successfully put forth multiple efforts to re-establish partnerships, ensure grant compliance, and increase enrollment and retention.

She also serves as an Adjunct Faculty at multiple institutions, where she facilitates and offers (online and classroom) instructions in the following areas: Preparation for Academic Achievement, Criminology, American Government, and State/Local Government, Public Policy Analysis, College Reading, Introduction to

Criminal Justice, and GED instruction. Additionally, Dr. Sinclaire has presented and facilitated instructions around the world on topics in the areas of succession planning, leadership, professional development, cohort learning, grant compliance, budget management, teamwork, civility, marketing, customer service, and self-defense.

She holds a Doctorate of Education from Mountaintop University in the Community College Leadership Doctoral Program, where she published dissertation research, "Maryland Community College Trustees' Intentions to Promote Succession Planning." She also maintains a Master of Science in Criminal Justice Administration and a Bachelor of Science Degree in Criminal Justice from Coppin State University.

Dr. Sinclaire is active in her community. She is a volunteer at the Archbishop Curley High School, a member of Delta Sigma Theta Sorority, Incorporated, and a member of the Faith United Baptist Church. She serves as a mentor for young adults, serves on the dance ministry, acts as a teenagers' counselor, and launched GED instructional programs in community churches throughout the city.

There're no better way to move on with life. Not minding what life throws at you, you should always be ready to make each moment count in your life. Try as much as you can not to be victim of circumstances and as well aim for your goal. God in His mercy will grant you mercy, grace, strength (resilience) to carry on. He is ever ready to help and to meet us at every point of our needs. Resilience from God is the ultimate! If He could do it for my sisters and I, you can't be left out.

LIFE WORTH LIVING

"The ultimate measure of a man is not where he stands in moments of comfort and convenience, but where he stands at times of challenge and controversy." – Dr. Martin Luther King.

Resilience has been defined as an attitude that enables the individual to examine, enhance, and utilize the strengths, characteristics, and other sources available to him or her.

It's a common fact that life is a wheel, sometimes we are up while sometimes we are down. Life is also a jungle out there, wherein you have to struggle for you to find your way out. Life can also be a battle, in which you have to fight hard so that you can survive. It can also be a journey where you have to withstand all your problems through thick and thin. But then again, in whatever way we may compare life, the most important thing is that we are resilient despite all the obstacles that may come.

Do we easily give up in life? How do we deal with our problems? Do we stand up and fight them? Do we learn from our problems? Or, do we back down and escape or run away from them?

Through the value of resilience, we can minimize stress and worries in our lives. We are also able to live a long, happy life in contentment and pleasure. With resilience in us, we do not quickly get burned out or pressured with the many different things that we do, such as with our jobs and with our responsibilities. Resilience also keeps us blooming, and it keeps us younger compared to our actual age. With resilience, we also become more enthusiastic and persevering towards life and all its challenges. Once again, with resilience, we are able to laugh at our problems or worries.

With it, we can cope or handle pressures and hassles smoothly or efficiently. Indeed, we can develop the value of resilience in many ways. One is when we do not simply give up with the different challenges that we may encounter in life. Another is when we develop or cultivate the right attitude and morals of goodness or kindness within us. When we become spiritually active, we are also able to strengthen the value of resilience within us. Next is also when we try to promote self-control or discipline in our daily life. Last is when we try to be enthusiastic with our actions and deeds, surely in this way we can glow inside and out.

Moreover, with resilience, we try to become more resilient and understanding. As the line goes, "Resilience is just another defense against the universe," we learn that with this value, we can come victorious in the battle of life. With resilience on us, we can make room for self- improvement. We are also made stronger by the value of resilience. Having resilience in our personality, we are able to spread our wings well. With this, we can bloom well and be the persons we are destined to be!

If you are facing adversity, tragedy or trauma here are secrets of resilient people.

- Resilient people don't focus on the dark side of a situation for very long. They maintain optimism and self-confidence. Whatever the challenge, they are sure that it can be overcome.
- Faith and spirituality matter to resilient people. They relinquish their adverse situation to a higher power allowing inner peace to flow.
- Resilient people are in constant pursuit of resolutions. They are not easily distracted, refusing to wallow in self-pity; instead, they spend time looking for answers.

- Resilient people wake up every day with grateful hearts. They focus on what they have as opposed to what they lack an understanding that challenges occur in life, and they can rise above the present struggle.
- Easily adaptable resilient people are masters of flexibility. Rolling with the punches, they adjust to challenging situations, which allows them to re-frame their thinking and move into action.

This list of resilient characteristics is not exhaustive, but it is a starting point for anyone who has experienced adversity, tragedy, or trauma. If you are feeling stuck but want to get your bounce back, remember resilience is about behavior and mindset, which means you can learn to do it. Happy Living!

REFERENCES

Benson H, Dusek JA, Sherwood JB, et al. (April 2006). "Study of the Therapeutic Effects of Intercessory Prayer (STEP) in cardiac bypass patients: a multicenter randomized trial of uncertainty and certainty of receiving intercessory prayer". American Heart Journal. 151 (4): 934–42. doi:10.1016/j.ahj.2005.05.028. PMID 16569567. Lay summary (PDF) – John Templeton Foundation (April 5, 2006).

Bradford, Sarah Hopkins (1961) [1886]. *Harriet Tubman: The Moses of Her People*. New York: Corinth Books. LCCN 61008152.

Charney, DS (2004). "Psychobiological mechanisms of resilience and vulnerability: implications for successful adaptation to extreme stress". Am J Psychiatry. 161 (2): 195–216. doi:10.1176/appi.ajp.161.2.195. PMID 14754765.

Clinton, Catherine (2004). Harriet Tubman: The Road to Freedom. New York: Little, Brown and Company. ISBN 0-316-14492-4.

Cohen, G. L., & Sherman, D. K. (2014). The psychology of change: Self-affirmation and social psychological intervention. Annual Review of Psychology, 65, 333-371

Cooper, Barry (Spring 2011). "Beethoven's

Uses of Silence". The Musical Times. 152 (1914): 25–43. JSTOR 23039954.

Creswell, J. D., Welch, W. T., Taylor, S. E., Sherman, D. K., Gruenewald, T. L., & Mann, T. (2005). Affirmation of personal values buffers neuroendocrine and psychological stress responses. Psychological Science, 16(11), 846-851.

Dan-Glauser, E. S.; Gross, J. J. (2011). "The temporal dynamics of two response-focused forms of emotion regulation: Experiential, expressive, and autonomic consequences". Psychophysiology. 48 (9): 1309–1322. doi:10.1111/j.1469-8986.2011.01191.x. PMC 3136552. PMID 21361967.

Emmons R.A. & McCullough, M.E. (2003). Counting Blessings versus Burdens: An experimental investiagation of gratitude and subjective well-being in daily life. Journal of personality and social psychology, 84, 377 – 389.

Emmons, R.A. (2008) Thanks! How The Science Of Gratitude Can Make You Happier. Mariner Book; Reprint edition.

Elfenbein, H. A.; Ambady, N. (2002). "On the universality and cultural specificity of emotion recognition: a meta-analysis". Psychological Bulletin. 128 (2): 203–235. doi:10.1037/0033-2909.128.2.203. PMID 11931516.

Greenberg, M.A. The Seven Best Attitude Quotes. Psychology Today.

Hobson, Janell (2014). "Between History and Fantasy: Harriet Tubman in the Artistic and Popular Imaginary". Meridians: Feminism, Race, Transnationalism. 12 (2): 50–77. doi:10.2979/meridians.

Leibovici, L (2001). "Effects of remote, retroactive intercessory prayer on outcomes in patients with bloodstream infection: randomized controlled trial". BMJ. 323 (7327): 1450–51. doi:10.1136/bmj.323.7327.1450. PMC 61047. PMID 11751349.

Lossef, N. and Doctor, J. (eds.) (2007) Silence, Music, Silent Music. London, Ashgate.

Luthar, S.S. (2006). "Resilience in development: A synthesis of research across five decades", pp. 739–795 in D. Cicchetti and D. J. Cohen (Eds.), Developmental Psychopathology (2nd ed.): Vol. 3 Risk, Disorder, and Adaptation. Hoboken, NJ: Wiley and Sons.

Mary Baker Eddy, "Prayer," in Science and Health with Key to the Scriptures, Boston, Trustees Under the Will of Mary Baker Eddy, 1934 [etc.] pp. 1–17.

Sherman, D. K., & Cohen, G. L. (2006). The psychology of self-defense: Self-affirmation theory. In M. P. Zanna (Ed.) Advances in experimental social psychology, 38, pp. 183-242. New York, NY: Guildford Press.

Sherman, D. K., Bunyan, D. P., Creswell, J.

D., & Jaremka, L. M. (2009). Psychological vulnerability and   stress: the effects of self-affirmation on sympathetic nervous system responses to naturalistic stressors. Health Psychology, 28(5), 554.

Siebert, Al (2005). The Resiliency Advantage, pp. 74–78. Berrett-Koehler Publishers. ISBN 1576753298.

Steele, C. M., Spencer, S. J., & Lynch, M. (1993). Self-image resilience and dissonance: the role of affirmational resources. Journal of Personality and Social Psychology, 64(6), 885.

Zautra, A.J., Hall, J.S. & Murray, K.E. (2010). "Resilience: A new definition of health for people and communities", pp. 3–34 in J.W. Reich, A.J. Zautra & J.S. Hall (eds.), Handbook of adult resilience. New York: Guilford, ISBN 146250647X.

www.ingramcontent.com/pod-product-compliance
Lightning Source LLC
Chambersburg PA
CBHW032105080426
42733CB00006B/424